HISTORIC CASTLES
OF BRITAIN

SUNBURST HERITAGE SERIES

HISTORIC CASTLES OF BRITAIN

GARRY GIBBONS

SUNBURST BOOKS

For Ria and Merry

The publishers would like to dedicate this title and the others in the series to Don Webb, to mark his contribution to the buying of books.

This edition first published 1994 by Sunburst Books, an imprint of the Promotional Reprint Company Limited, Deacon House, 65 Old Church Street, London SW3 5BS

Designed by Anthony Cohen
Printed and bound in China

ISBN 1 85778 048 5

Cover photograph: Langley Castle, Northumberland
Half title: Old Scotney Castle, Kent
Title page: Windsor Castle, Berkshire

CONTENTS

Introduction 6

ENGLAND

WALES

SCOTLAND

INTRODUCTION

Castles differ enormously. From the great baronial battlements built to dominate the surrounding landscape to the modest fortified manor house, the castles of Britain share one common factor - the balance between stronghold and residence. This balance was struck according to the rank of the owner, the region and the period in which the castle was raised.

The castle emerged as a means of supporting the feudal system. The word feudal comes from the Latin *feodum*, meaning a fee or payment, and was designed to bind society together like a pyramid with the king at its apex.

In short, all land belonged to the king but to defend and administer his kingdom he required assistance. This was achieved by granting parcels of land to barons in return for agreed services to the crown. The barons retained portions of that land and distributed the remainder to their followers. At the base of the pyramid came the peasants, smallholders who worked the lord's land for an agreed number of days. The land remaining directly under the king's control was administered by his representatives, the constables, from the security of the royal castles.

Although fewer in number than all the baronial castles, the royal castles exceeded those owned by any one baron. The feudal castle provided a power base for both the king and his barons, from which they could administer authority, justice and law enforcement. Although often abused, the feudal system survived for 400 years from its beginnings under the Normans.

Castle building began abruptly with the arrival on the Sussex coast of William, Duke of Normandy. Upon landing, his first act was to build a castle at Pevensey. This strategy of constructing a forward base, and thereby securing territory during a general advance, was to ensure William's conquest of Britain following his victory over the Saxon King, Harold, on 14th October, 1066.

Immediately following his coronation, William

had the country surveyed and set about a massive castle-building programme. Five years after the Conquest William had established thirty-three castles, and by his death in 1087 that number had risen to eighty-six.

Those early castles took the form of a wooden building comprising a kitchen, well and sleeping accommodation for the men and horses; a hall on the first floor for security; storerooms and workshops and, usually, a chapel. This building, or keep, was surrounded by a high wooden fence atop a bank, which in turn was encircled by a ditch. The whole defensive area was known as the bailey.

This basic structure developed over time as the timber buildings became more complex and were placed on mounds, or mottes. Access was by means of a flying bridge, which was protected by a wooden palisade. The timber watchtower and fence were often rebuilt in stone to increase the castle's defences. This stronghold with a stone outer wall became known as a shell keep.

No English account describing the construction of a motte-and-bailey exists, however a document that details the building of a similar French castle has been passed down from circa 1130:

> It is the custom of the nobles of that neighbourhood to make a mound of earth as high as they can and dig about it as wide and deep as possible. The space on top of the mound is enclosed by a palisade of very strong hewn logs, strengthened at intervals by as many towers as their means can provide. Inside the enclosure is a citadel, or keep, which commands the whole circuit of the defences. The entrance to the fortress is by means of a bridge which, arising from the outer side of the moat, and supported by posts as it ascends, reaches the top of the mound.

Generally, the motte-and-bailey castle could be erected quite rapidly and improvements added as time and resources allowed. Unfortunately, the timber keep which was the heart of the castle was prone to destruction, as much by rot as by fire. The effects of rot could be delayed by raising the wooden building on stone sleeper-walls, however the spread of the rectangular stone keep, like that at Castle Rising, Norfolk (see pages 36/37), marked the eventual demise of the early timber structures.

A rapid increase in private strongholds presented the need for a strong king to control his barons and their castle-building activities. From early Norman times, no stronghold could be built without royal consent. These licences to crenellate, or build a structure with battlements, were granted to trusted followers and family, although this by no means guaranteed their continuing loyalty.

Norman influence spread into Wales by the tried and tested pattern of domination. The first task was to secure the Welsh Marches (from the French *marche*, meaning frontier) by means of the motte-and-bailey castle. From these bases, the Norman lords soon occupied much of south Wales and, to a lesser extent, the northern coastline.

From their heartland in Snowdonia, the Welsh mounted a campaign of resistance against the Normans in a series of hit-and-run raids. This action brought the latest innovations in castle design into the area, which the Welsh princes would often imitate. Eventually both the Normans and the Welsh had strongholds scattered liberally across their respective territories.

Feudalism and castle building came to Scotland later and at a more gradual pace. The death of William Canmore in 1093 caused great upheaval, resulting in his sons, Alexander and David, seeking refuge in the Norman courts of England. Eventually returning to rule Scotland through the first half of the 12th century, they would encourage the 'bloodless Norman conquest'.

Alexander's reign saw the slow introduction of Norman retainers, but, following David's succession to the throne, the process of Normanisation greatly expanded. Through the increase of feudal ties and landholding, supported by the royal castles, David reasserted the power of the monarchy, much as the Normans had done with such success throughout England.

Here, then, immediately following the Norman Conquest, is the period which laid the foundations for the Medieval castle, whose legacy has provided us with a staggering display of grandeur and whose diversity is celebrated over the following pages.

Garry Gibbons, January 1994

ENGLAND

Main photograph: POWDERHAM CASTLE, DEVON
A fortified manor house dating from 1390, which was built to command the Exeter estuary by
Sir Phillip Courtenay, ancestor of the Earls of Devon. Following a siege in the Civil War, the
castle required substantial alterations and further restoration work has been carried out recently.
Powderham remains home to the Courtenay family.

Inset photograph: DUNSTER CASTLE, SOMERSET
Over its 900 year history Dunster Castle has been home to two families. Shortly after the
Norman Conquest, William de Mohun built a wooden stronghold on the site, which was replaced
by a stone structure in the 12th century. The castle passed into the Luttrell family in 1404 and
subsequently fell into disrepair, remaining in this state until extensive refurbishments by George

Main photograph: PENDENNIS CASTLE
and, inset: ST MAWES CASTLE, CORNWALL
Two forts in a chain of defences built under Henry VIII, which stretches along
England's south coast to guard against invasion. St Mawes, of lobate design, has
remained unchanged since it was completed in 1543, whereas Pendennis Castle,
standing on the opposite shore, was substantially enlarged during the reign of
Elizabeth I. Both castles were designed to defend the Carrick Roads estuary,
Falmouth harbour and the Cornish mainland by means of a lethal web of crossfire.

Main photograph: BROUGHTON CASTLE, OXFORDSHIRE
A fortified manor house surrounded by a broad moat, the castle was built by Sir John de Broughton around 1300. Although substantially enlarged in 1550, the medieval building survives behind the Tudor facade. The castle remains home to Lord and Lady Saye and Sele and has been in their family for the past 600 years.

Inset photograph: BERKELEY CASTLE, GLOUCESTERSHIRE
Robert Fitzharding was made lord of Berkeley by Henry II in the 1150s, and with the title came lands and a Norman timber castle. Robert soon set about improving the stronghold by erecting a stone wall around both the mound and castle, creating an extremely rare form of shell keep. The great hall and chapel were included in an extensive building programme from 1340-1350. Berkeley was the scene of Edward II's gruesome murder, when a red hot poker was thrust "through the secret place posterial." Berkeley Castle remains home to the descendants of Robert Fitzharding

NUNNEY CASTLE, WILTSHIRE

Built by Sir John de la Mare on his return from the French wars in 1373. The site lay below the village of
Nunney within the grounds of his native manor. The four-storey tower house is surrounded on three sides by a
moat and on the fourth by the village stream. The castle survived until September 1645, when it was con-
demned to ruin

Main photograph and inset: OLD WARDOUR CASTLE, WILTSHIRE
Built in 1393 for John, fifth Lord Lovel, Old Wardour is a fortress residence in the French style. During the
late 16th century Sir Mathew Arundell ordered the reconstruction of the castle, which was undertaken by the
leading Elizabethan architect, Robert Smythson. Old Wardour was badly damaged during the Civil War and
eventually abandoned by the Arundell family in the 18th century.

FARLEIGH HUNGERFORD CASTLE, SOMERSET
The construction of this castle was started in the 1370s by Sir Thomas Hungerford, first recorded Speaker of the House of Commons, merchant prince and Chief Steward of John of Gaunt's land south of the River Trent. Work was completed around 1383, when Sir Thomas was granted a pardon for proceeding with construction of the castle without the appropriate permission. The castle was enlarged by his son, Sir Walter Hungerford, a notable soldier under Henry V.

Main photograph: ARUNDEL CASTLE, WEST SUSSEX
Seat of the Earls of Norfolk and their ancestors for over 700 years, the castle was built by Roger de Montgomery, Earl of Arundel, at the end of the 11th century. Most of the original work was carried out under the direction of William d'Albini, who was responsible for a number of stone keeps, including Castle Riding, Norfolk (see pages 36/37). In 1580 the estate passed to the Dukes of Norfolk by way of marriage. The castle was severely damaged in 1643 and remained uninhabitable until restoration work in the 18th and 19th centuries.

Inset photograph: HERSTMONCEUX CASTLE, EAST SUSSEX
 Early in the 13th century the old manor house which stood upon this site belonged to the de Hurst family, who would later add the surname of de Monceux to their own. By 1331 the property had passed to the de Fiennes, and by the early part of the 15th century Roger de Fiennes raised the present rectangular brick castle. In 1441 a licence was granted to John de Fiennes to "... enclose, crenellate and furnish with towers his manor of Herst Monceux".

20

PORTCHESTER CASTLE, HAMPSHIRE

The Normans built a small castle here within the abandoned remains of a Roman fort. The huge walls surrounding the site are interrupted at regular intervals by mural towers with Norman gateways on the east and west sides. The Norman keep dates from the 12th century, when the castle was used as a departure point for armies bound for France. With the rise in importance of nearby Portsmouth, Portchester Castle gradually fell into decline during the 15th century.

HEVER CASTLE, KENT

A manor house dating from 1270, the first fortifications were added after a licence had been granted around 1340. A further licence granted to Sir John de Cobhan in 1384 saw the construction of the main defences and moating. In 1462 Hever was purchased by a London trader and former Lord Mayor of London, Sir Geoffrey Boleyn, whose daughter Anne was the second wife of Henry VIII and mother to Elizabeth I. After Sir Geoffrey's death, Henry gave the castle to his fourth and recently divorced wife, Anne of Cleeves. Hever Castle later fell into ruin until its restoration by William Waldorf Astor in 1903.

BODIAM CASTLE, EAST SUSSEX
Bodiam is perhaps the finest surviving example of a 14th century castle in Britain. Its builder, Sir Edward Dalyngrigge, was one of England's great patriots, whose fame and fortune was founded on the French campaigns under Edward III. Sir Edward gained the estate at Bodiam through marriage, and, by a licence of 1386, was granted permission to fortify the manor house. However, this proved to be impractical, so a new castle was constructed. Bodiam escaped the ravages of the Civil War and, although falling into ruin, was restored in 1917.

OLD SCOTNEY CASTLE, KENT

In the Middle Ages, as a result of growing fear of attack following French action in the English Channel, wealthy landowners and retired military men in the south east of England were encouraged by the crown to fortify manors or build castles. Around 1378 the manor house at Scotney was fortified by its owner, Roger de Ashburnham, a prominent local administrator and Conservator of the Peace in Kent and Sussex along with Sir John de Etchingham and Sir Edward Dalyngrigge, who would later build Bodiam Castle (see pages 26/27). Old Scotney today comprises a 17th century house along with a portion of the original castle.

LEEDS CASTLE, KENT
Built across two islands with a lake and a woodland backdrop, Leeds is one of England's most picturesque castles. The original structure was completed by Edward I sometime in the 1270s and given to his Queen, Elenor. Leeds then became part of the dower of English queens until the 15th century. Despite its conversion to a Tudor palace by Henry VIII, Leeds Castle owes its present 'medieval' appearance to extensive rebuilding and restoration work carried out in the 19th and 20th centuries.

England's first rectangular stone keep dating from about 1079, White Tower was the work of master builder, Gandalf, who dominated the second phase of castle building under the Normans as stone replaced wood. The walls, built of Caen stone, are approximately 3.7 meters thick at the base. The distinctive corner cupolas were added in the 14th century.

The inner curtain wall was begun under Henry III and completed by Edward I, who also started work on the outer defensive wall. Further remodelling was carried out by Henry VIII.

Main photograph: ROUND TOWER, WINDSOR CASTLE, BERKSHIRE

The huge mound is of natural chalk, a perfect choice for the location of a Thameside keep. Built soon after the Norman Conquest by William I, it may have been constructed from stone at the outset, as the mound is capable of withstanding the tremendous weight. Henry I held court there in 1114, with Henry II adding halls and offices to accommodate his court around 1175. In 1826 the tower was refaced in stone and raised to its present height of about 20 meters. The Round Tower is photographed from the Upper Ward.

Inset photograph: STATE APARTMENTS, WINDSOR CASTLE

The state apartments form the Upper Ward of Windsor and owe much of their appearance to 19th century building work. Built originally by Henry II, the apartments have seen many changes over the centuries, most notably those instigated by Edward III, Charles II and George III.

Main photograph: ST GEORGE'S CHAPEL, WINDSOR CASTLE
Edward III will be remembered above all as the founder of the Order of the Garter, the oldest and most
renowned of the Orders of chivalry. For its first 135 years the Order was housed in an early chapel built by
Henry III. It was in need of frequent repair and, by 1478, Edward IV resolved to replace it. The result is
St George's Chapel, a masterpiece in Perpendicular Gothic.

Inset photograph: THE EAST FACE, WINDSOR CASTLE
The earliest stone work of the two central towers dates from the time of Henry II. Originally watch towers,
they were enlarged by Edward III to provide living accommodation. Forming the outer walls of the state apart-

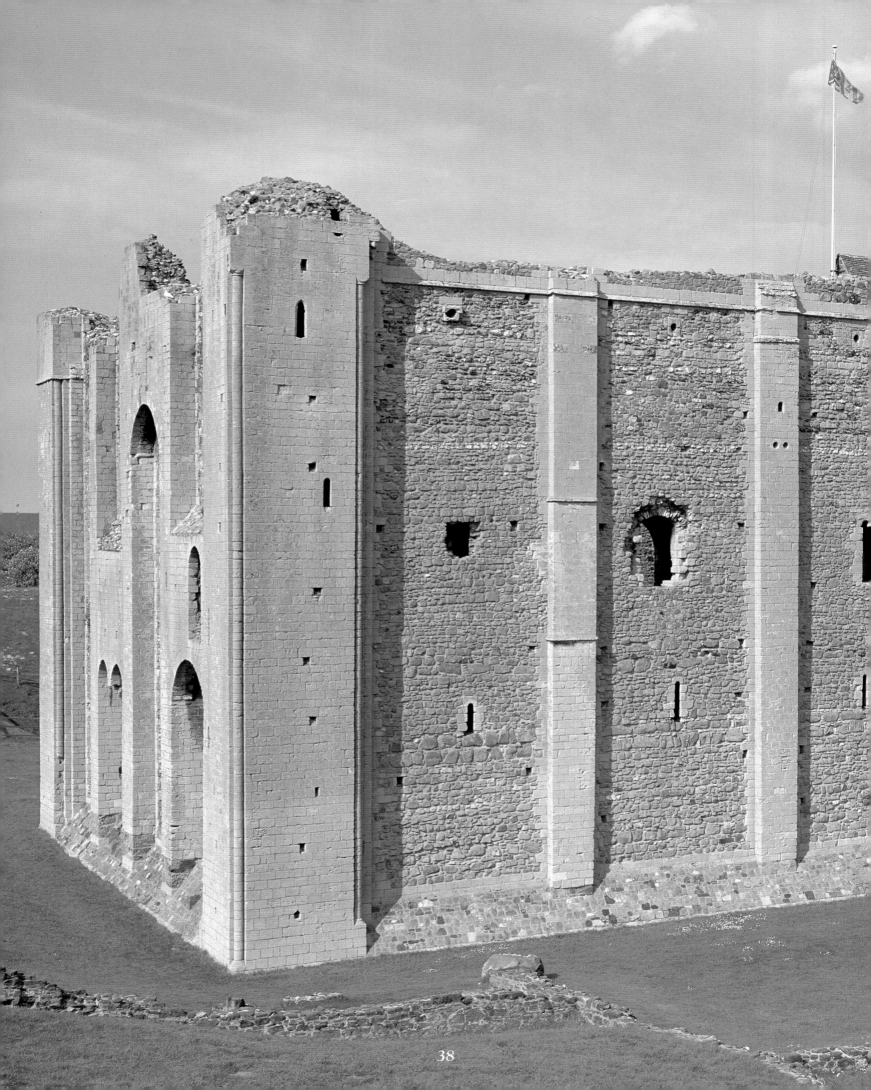

CASTLE RISING, NORFOLK

Confiscated by William I, the site at Castle Rising was given to his half brother, Odo, Bishop of Bayeux. The land later passed to William d'Albini, whose son built the massive stone keep around 1140. The castle later passed to the crown and from 1331-1351 Queen Isabella, Edward II's widow, lived there.

WARWICK CASTLE, WARWICKSHIRE

The early tower of 1068 is said to have been demolished in 1264 by partisans of Simon de Montford, Earl of Leicester, who "... beat down the wall from tower to tower." The magnificent structure that stands there today is the work of the Beauchamp family, the Earls of Warwick, and dates mainly from the 14th century. Started by Thomas Beauchamp, building continued after his death in 1369 and was completed by his son in 1394. The castle and title passed to the Neville family in the 15th century and about 200 years later James I gave it to Sir Fulk Greville, who erected the state apartments.

BADDESLEY CLINTON, WARWICKSHIRE

A medieval moated manor house dating in part from the 14th century, although much work was carried out a century later by its owner, John Brome, and his son, Nicholas. In 1517 the house passed via Nicholas's daughter to her husband, Sir Edward Ferrers, and remained in his family until 1884. The manor house has seen little

LUDLOW CASTLE, SHROPSHIRE

Once the administrative headquarters of Wales and the Marches, Ludlow Castle stands high overlooking the River Teme and dates from the 11th century. The original walled enclosure, four square towers and gatehouse now form the inner bailey of this large and imposing castle. A Yorkist stronghold during the Wars of the Roses, Ludlow fell into disrepair until it passed to the Earls of Powis.

KENILWORTH CASTLE, WARWICKSHIRE

A mighty castle which suffered at the hands of Parliament and now stands as a glorious ruin. Begun in the 12th century by Geoffrey de Clinton, Kenilworth was enlarged a century later by King John. Soon after the castle endured a six month siege, but eventually the occupants fell victim to starvation. Over the following centuries John of Gaunt, Duke of Lancaster and Robert Dudley, Earl of Leicester transformed Kenilworth Castle into a grand palace fit to entertain the royal court.

STOKESAY CASTLE, SHROPSHIRE

A rare example of a fortified medieval house that has survived with very few alterations. Stokesay stood as a hall and tower structure when it was purchased in 1281 by Lawrence of Ludlow, a local wool merchant. By 1291 Lawrence was granted a licence for further defences, adding the large south tower and private chambers. Descendants of Lawrence remained at Stokesay for 300 years until the Cravens took over. The property was let as a farm and workshop in the 18th century. Stokesay Castle was sold in 1869 and restored to its present condition.

ASHBY-DE-LA-ZOUCH CASTLE, LEICESTERSHIRE

The old manor house of Ashby was inherited by William, first Lord Hastings, a man of considerable wealth and power. A licence to crenellate the old manor house was granted in April, 1474. In the same year William entered into an agreement with two lords, nine knights and forty-eight squires, who pledged to aid him against all persons within the kingdom and to raise as many men as possible at William's expense. Lord Hastings' tragic end, when he was seized during a meeting of the Privy Council, taken out and beheaded, is described in Shakespeare's *Richard II*.

DUNSTANBURGH CASTLE, NORTHUMBERLAND
The approach to the castle along a windswept coastline emphasises the remote silhouettes that are the remains of Dunstanburgh. It was built after the English defeat at Bannockburn by Thomas, Earl of Lancaster, between 1313 and 1322 as a defence against the raiding Scots army. Dunstanburgh stands isolated on an island created by a man-made ditch some 80 meters wide. Further additions were carried out by John of Gaunt around 1380 and the castle remained an important border fortress until the Tudor period.

Main photograph: ALNWICK CASTLE, NORTHUMBERLAND
A stone keep from 1095 was the first fortification on this site. Built by the de Vescis family, its history was
untroubled until the 14th century heralded a fresh outbreak of wars between the English and the Scots.
Having purchased the castle from the Bishop of Durham in 1309, the Percy family set about enlarging the
stronghold, and although the power of the Percys diminished during the Tudor period, their descendants, the
Dukes of Northumberland, ensured that the castle remained as a great family seat.

Inset photograph: WARKWORTH CASTLE, NORTHUMBERLAND
A further testimony to the power of the Percy family throughout the north of England. The Percys purchased
the existing 12th century castle in 1332 and set about building a massive tower-keep and developing the
defences. The demise of power for the Percy family began after an unsuccessful attempt to unseat Henry IV, as
a result of which the king marched on Warkworth and forced its surrender in 1405. The Percys did eventually
return to their favourite castle.

HARLECH CASTLE, GWYNEDD

Harlech stands on a commanding position atop a high crag overlooking Tremadog Bay, and although it was once at the sea's edge, the castle now lies some distance inland. Built between May, 1285 and December, 1291, Harlech shares with Beaumaris Castle the tactical strength of the concentric design, allowing forces on the castle's inner ring of defences to defend the outer wall. Thus in 1294 thirty-seven men defended Harlech Castle against the entire Welsh army and in the early 1400s the castle withstood siege by Owen Glendower with a force of only forty men (the famous, 'Men of Harlech'), falling only after the French fleet cut off the

BEAUMARIS CASTLE, ANGLESEY, GWYNEDD

Beaumaris (beautiful marsh) is considered the ultimate 'concentric' castle - its geometric design and outer circuit of defences combine an enormous level of firepower and security. Begun in 1295, this is the last and largest in the series of fortifications raised by Edward I, and although vast quantities of money and manpower were lavished on Beaumaris, building work slowed and finally stopped in 1343, leaving the castle unfinished but habitable.

Main photograph: KIDWELLY CASTLE, DYFED
 An early stronghold was built on this site soon after 1106 by Bishop Roger of Salisbury as part of a chain of such castles intended to defend important coastal routes. By the late 13th century Kidwelly was held by Payn de Chaworth, who set about rebuilding the castle in stone in the 1270s, following a series of attacks by the Welsh. Further alterations were carried out over the next 300 years under Henry of Lancaster and Sir Rhys ap Thomas. By the 17th century Kidwelly was "utterly ruyned and decayed."

Inset photograph: MANORBIER CASTLE, DYFED
"the most delightful part of Pembroch ... the pleasantest place in Wales" wrote Gerald of Wales (1146?-1220?) about his birthplace, Manorbier Castle. Like Kidwelly Castle, Manorbier was a Norman stronghold built in wood until the powerful de Barri family began a programme of rebuilding in stone throughout the 12th century.

CAREW CASTLE, DYFED
Building at Carew began towards the end of the 13th century, replacing an earlier Norman fortification on this site. During the 15th century the castle was greatly enlarged, in particular by the addition of the great hall. The role of Carew was gradually changing from that of castle to a luxurious Tudor mansion, which was later completely refurbished by Sir John Perrot, reputedly Henry VIII's natural son.

Main photograph: PEMBROKE CASTLE, DYFED
Birthplace in 1457 of Henry VII, the first of the Tudor dynasty, Pembroke Castle stands high on its rocky promontory overlooking Milford Haven. The castle's history began in 1090, when Arnulf of Montgomery raised a small bailey which was to withstand a lengthy siege by the Welsh. Complete reconstruction of the castle was undertaken in the late 12th century by William Marshal, son-in-law of Strongbow, the conqueror of Ireland. During the Civil War, Pembroke was the location of conflict between the Royalists and Roundheads, with Cromwell himself leading an attack against what he described as "a very desperate enemy .. and one of the strongest places in the country."

Inset photograph: PICTON CASTLE, DYFED
An imposing Edwardian castle, which was started in the 13th century by Sir John Wogan, Justiciar of Ireland, under Edward I. Picton then passed to the Dwnn family, and, later in the 15th century, through marriage to the Philipps, whose descendants still own the castle. Several additions were made to the castle in the 1800s, and during its recent past it has been restored as a modern residence.

CHEPSTOW CASTLE, GWENT

Built by William FitzOsbern before his death in 1071, Chepstow was designed as part of his expansion into Wales. The castle commands the junction of the rivers Wye and Severn, a vital river crossing into south Wales. FitzOsbern constructed his rectangular hall-keep in stone, making it one of the earliest of its type. Chepstow underwent further development under William Marshal after he became lord in 1189, and his son completed the castle's basic layout as we see it today. Further additions were made by Roger Bigod, Earl of Norfolk, in the 14th century. The castle saw little action until the Civil War, after which it was left to decay.

Main photograph: CALDICOT CASTLE, GWENT
Following the Norman Conquest, Caldicot passed from Durand, Sheriff of Gloucester, to the Norman family of de Bohun, Earls of Hereford, who held the castle until 1377. During the course of the Bohun ownership, Caldicot was substantially extended and rebuilt in stone. The Great Gatehouse dates from the 14th century and is considered to be the finest example of architecture in the castle. Caldicot next fell to Thomas of Woodstock, Duke of Gloucester, the youngest son of Edward III, who was tragically murdered in 1398. Finally the castle came under the control of the ducal house of Buckingham, which ended in 1521, when Edward Stafford, third Duke of Buckingham, fell victim to Henry VIII's jealousy.

Inset photograph: PENHOW CASTLE, GWENT
A small fortified manor house that is supposed to be the oldest inhabited castle in Wales. Its courtyard contains some fine examples of architecture, reflecting its 800 year history.

Main photograph: RAGLAN CASTLE, GWENT
The great castle-palace home to the Somersets, Earls of Worcester, fell to the Parliamentary forces in 1646 during the Civil War. The Earl was taken into custody, dying some months later. All items of value, including the great library, which contained many ancient Welsh manuscripts, were burnt under the direction of Henry Herbert, direct descendant of William ap Thomas, who founded Raglan around 1435. William built the massive hexagonal keep known as the 'Yellow Tower of Gwent' and his son, Sir William Herbert, later Earl of Pembroke, continued work on the castle following his father's death.

Inset photograph: WHITE CASTLE, GWENT
One of three important castles that controlled the southern Marches. The curtain wall and moat date from 1184-86. By 1254 the castle belonged to Lord Edward, later Edward I, and in 1267 it passed to his younger brother, Edmund, Earl of Lancaster. During this period the gatehouse and circular towers were added as defensive measures in response to the threatening power of Llywelyn ap Gruffudd. White Castle takes its name from the plaster which covered its walls and towers.

CAERPHILLY CASTLE, MID GLAMORGAN

A high point of medieval military architecture, Caerphilly Castle stands surrounded by its huge system of defences covering some 30 acres. Building work began in April, 1268 under the instructions of the powerful Marcher lord, Earl Gilbert de Clare, only to fall to Llywelyn ap Gruffydd some two years later. In 1326 major rebuilding work and additions were ordered by Hugh le Despenser the younger, who acquired the castle after marriage to a de Clare heiress. Edward II took refuge at Caerphilly following the invasion led by his exiled Queen, Isabella, "the She Wolf of France." Edward was eventually captured and the castle surrendered soon afterwards. By Tudor times the castle had fallen into decay and remained so until its restoration in the 19th century.

SCOTLAND

EILEAN DONAN CASTLE, HIGHLANDS

Standing on an island at the junction of three lochs, Eilean Donan Castle was constructed by Alexander II in 1220 as a defence against the Danes. Whilst held by the Jacobites in 1719, it was heavily bombarded by an English warship and lay in ruins until its restoration in 1932.

DUNVEGAN CASTLE, ISLE OF SKYE

Seat of the chiefs of MacLeod for over 700 years, Dunvegan remains the MacLeod family home to this day.
One of the many precious relics housed at Dunvegan is the Fairy Flag, an ancient cloth reputed to possess magical powers, which could be harnessed to save the clan if the flag was waved in times of great need.

CRAIGIEVAR CASTLE, GRAMPIAN

Set in the Grampian countryside, Craigievar Castle consists of a string of tower houses, each of which is a fine example of the Scottish Baronial style. The upright construction and relatively small ground surface area were deliberately designed as defence against local skirmishes. Today Craigievar stands in much the same state as it

Main photograph: FYVIE CASTLE, GRAMPIAN
Fyvie Castle is considered the crowning glory of the tower house, with its five imposing towers, each of which
represents one of the dynasties which have owned the castle during its 500 year history — the Prestons,
the Meldrums, the Setons, the Gordons and the Leiths.

Inset photograph: CASTLE FRASER, GRAMPIAN
Craigievar Castle was designed on an L-shaped plan, whilst its close neighbour, Castle Fraser, is based on the
Z-shaped plan, each of which was common in the later, more complex style of tower house which could
accommodate the addition of various wings. Castle Fraser was built around the original five-storey round tower
and completed for Michael Fraser in 1636.

BLAIR CASTLE, TAYSIDE

Home to the Atholl family for 700 years, Blair Castle is assured of a place in Scottish history. Built around the earlier structure known as Comyn's Tower in 1269, Blair has continued to expand over the centuries despite siege and capture. The castle fell to Cromwell's troops during the Civil War and the Atholls were later rewarded by Queen Anne, who created the 2nd marquess, Duke of Atholl, in 1703. Blair became the last private castle to be besieged in Britain during the Jacobite rebellion, when Lord George Murray, who forfeited his inheritance by supporting Bonnie Prince Charlie, laid siege to his own home.

CASTLE STALKER, STRATHCLYDE

A rectangular keep set on a rocky island, Castle Stalker has looked out across Loch Laich since the 13th century, when it was built by the Stewarts of Appin. Ownership by the Stewarts was put to the test during one particularly merry revel in 1689 when the castle's owner exchanged the stronghold for a small galley, doubtless while he was under the influence of the castle's fine cellar.

KILCHURN CASTLE, STRATHCLYDE

Kilchurn Castle stands on a spit of land extending out into Loch Awe, Scotland's longest loch. It was the stronghold of Sir Colin Campbell, and dates from the 15th century, although additions to the structure were made in 1693 by John Campbell, 1st Earl of Breadalbane. The castle was eventually abandoned in the middle of the

Main photograph: EDINBURGH CASTLE, LOTHIAN
Standing high on a crag of volcanic rock, Edinburgh Castle dominates its city. Although fortifications have existed here since the Iron Age, the castle's association with royalty began in the 11th century, when Edinburgh became the principal royal residence during the reign of Malcolm Canmore. Over the following 700 years the castle changed hands as a consequence of the Anglo-Scottish wars, falling to the Earl of Moray in 1313, who dismantled the castle under orders from Robert the Bruce; to Cromwell after severe bombardment in 1650; to William of Orange in 1689; finally, the castle withstood a blockade during the ill-fated rebellion led by Bonnie Prince Charlie.

Inset photograph: STIRLING CASTLE, CENTRAL
The appearance and history of Stirling Castle shares many similarities with Edinburgh Castle. Known as the 'key to Scotland' the castle stands guard over the main route running between north and south. The castle we see today dates from the 15th and 16th centuries, although the earlier fortification was dismantled on the orders of Robert the Bruce. Stirling was the birthplace of James III in 1451, and the young Mary Queen of Scots was crowned here in December, 1543.

CAWDOR CASTLE, HIGHLANDS
The special licence granted by James II to his friend, William, Thane of Cawdor, in 1454 permitted him to erect and fortify his castle "..with walls and ditches and equip the summit with turrets and means of defence, with warlike provisions and strengths." The buildings that surround the original five-storey tower date from the 17th century.

Inset photograph: **CASTLE STUART, HIGHLANDS**
At the start of the construction of this castle in 1621, the Royal House of Stuart had ruled England, Wales, Ireland and Scotland for about twenty years. Ancient home to the Earls of Moray and the Stuart family, the castle stands within range of the sound of the roar of cannons from Culloden Moor, site of the final battle in the rebellion led by Bonnie Prince Charlie in his bid to restore the Stuart monarchy.

KELLIE CASTLE, FIFE

Built around an original 14th century keep, Kellie has evolved into a fine laird's house. Originally home to the Oliphant family, the castle passed to the Earls of Nar and Kellie in 1613. A period of neglect ended in the late 19th century when a lease was granted to the Lorimer family, whose gradual restoration ensured the rescue of this unspoilt example of 16th and 17th century traditional Scottish architecture.

Main photograph: CRICHTON CASTLE, LOTHIAN
Originally built by John de Crichton, but considerably enlarged by his son, William, in the 15th century, Crichton
Castle stands above a charming valley overlooking the River Tyne. Crichton later became part of the Bothwell earl-
dom until the mid 16th century, when it was completely refurbished after passing to Francis Stewart.

Inset photograph: HERMITAGE CASTLE, BORDERS
Amongst the most renowned of the border fortresses, Hermitage Castle stands as a forbidding reminder of a treacher-
ous past, having been held successively by the families of Soulis, Dacre, Douglas and Bothwell. The fifth Earl of
Bothwell was visited by his future wife, Mary Queen of Scots, in October, 1566, as he lay wounded at Hermitage.

HISTORIC CASTLES
OF BRITAIN

76

74

90 90

80

78 80

82

84

86

92

88

88

94

GLASGOW ● EDINBURGH ●

94

52

54 54

NEWCASTLE

LEEDS

MANCHESTER

58

56

50

38

BIRMINGHAM

48

44

46

42 40

12

70

50

64

62 60

70

66 12

64

60

SWANSEA

72

68

68

32

34

LONDON

CARDIFF

BRISTOL

18

30

8

14

24

28

26

16

20

22

20

8

10 10

© The Automobile Association 1994